ORCA

'Does the sea frighten you? Your boat is very small. Do you know your friends well? Are they good at sailing?'

Jack, his wife Tonya, and his friends Max and Sasha want to sail from England to Australia. They have a lot of money and they don't want to work any more – they want an exciting life.

And it is exciting for them. And at first everything is easy. But an exciting life can also be a dangerous life. The sea is not always a friendly place – and when you need help, you need good friends and a lot of luck.

LONDON BOROUGH OF BARNET

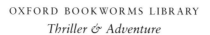

OXFORD BOOKWORMS LIBRARY
Thriller & Adventure

Orca

Starter (250 headwords)

PHILLIP BURROWS AND MARK FOSTER

Orca

OXFORD UNIVERSITY PRESS

OXFORD

UNIVERSITY PRESS

Great Clarendon Street, Oxford OX2 6DP

Oxford University Press is a department of the University of Oxford.
It furthers the University's objective of excellence in research, scholarship,
and education by publishing worldwide in

Oxford New York

Auckland Cape Town Dar es Salaam Hong Kong Karachi
Kuala Lumpur Madrid Melbourne Mexico City Nairobi
New Delhi Shanghai Taipei Toronto

With offices in

Argentina Austria Brazil Chile Czech Republic France Greece
Guatemala Hungary Italy Japan Poland Portugal Singapore
South Korea Switzerland Thailand Turkey Ukraine Vietnam

OXFORD and OXFORD ENGLISH are registered trade marks of
Oxford University Press in the UK and in certain other countries

This edition © Oxford University Press 2008

The moral rights of the author have been asserted

Database right Oxford University Press (maker)

First published in Oxford Bookworms 2004

12 14 16 18 20 19 17 15 13 11

No unauthorized photocopying

All rights reserved. No part of this publication may be reproduced,
stored in a retrieval system, or transmitted, in any form or by any means,
without the prior permission in writing of Oxford University Press,
or as expressly permitted by law, or under terms agreed with the appropriate
reprographics rights organization. Enquiries concerning reproduction
outside the scope of the above should be sent to the ELT Rights Department,
Oxford University Press, at the address above

You must not circulate this book in any other binding or cover
and you must impose this same condition on any acquirer

Any websites referred to in this publication are in the public domain and
their addresses are provided by Oxford University Press for information only.
Oxford University Press disclaims any responsibility for the content

ISBN: 978 0 19 423424 5

A complete recording of this Bookworms edition of
Orca is available in an audio pack. ISBN 978 0 19 423447 4

Printed in China

Word count (main text): 1600

For more information on the Oxford Bookworms Library, visit
www.oup.com/elt/gradedreaders

This book is printed on paper from certified and well-managed sources.

CONTENTS

1 Let's do it!

Jack Griggs stands on his boat. The wind is strong and his boat moves quickly over the sea. A big, white bird goes past and makes a noise. 'Keyaaaa', it cries.

Jack smiles and says: 'Hello, bird. How are you, today?'

Jack's friends laugh and give some fish to the bird.

'Ah,' says Jack. 'Hungry, I see.' Jack's friends are Max and Sasha, and his wife's name is Tonya.

'I am hungry, too,' says Jack. 'Sandwiches and drinks everybody? Tonya. Can you steer?'

Half an hour later they are eating. 'What are we going to do now?' asks Jack.

'Oh, I am going to read my book. Then I'm going to sleep,' says Tonya.

'No – what about tomorrow? . . . Next month? . . . Next year?' Jack looks at everyone. 'We have lots of money from our old business, but . . .'

'We can start another business,' says Max.

'A sailing business?' says Sasha.

'I don't want to work any more,' says Tonya. 'We don't need to work.'

'OK, listen to me,' says Jack. 'I am thinking about sailing around the world.'

Max, Tonya and Sasha look at Jack. 'What? From here to Australia?' says Tonya.

'Of course,' says Jack. He is getting very excited now. 'Max, what do you think?'

'I think we must talk about it,' says Max.

They talk for hours. It is night when Max, Sasha and Tonya say excitedly: 'OK. Let's do it!'

They have to do a lot before they leave. Jack talks to a man who knows about sailing around the world. He tells Jack that it is hard work.

'Does the sea frighten you? Your boat is very small. Do you know your friends well? Are they good at sailing?' he asks.

'We know each other well. They are the best people in the world,' says Jack.

The four friends look at lots of maps. Sasha wants to see a whale. Max wants to see Africa. 'I want to sit in the sun and catch fish to eat,' laughs Tonya.

It is exciting for all of them. And at first everything is easy.

The big day arrives – they are leaving. Some of their friends and family come to watch. Their friends stand by the water and say goodbye.

'Good luck,' one of them says.

'Don't forget us!' says Sasha's sister.

'Write to me every day,' says Tonya's friend. 'Give the letters to a bird.'

Sasha begins to cry. 'What are we doing? Do I really want to go?' she thinks. Max takes her hand. All of them are quiet, excited, and a little unhappy.

'Bye,' says Jack quietly.

2 Sailing south

The wind is strong and the boat moves faster and faster. Jack, Max, Sasha and Tonya are happy at sea. There is a lot to do on the boat. The wind is behind them and soon they cannot see England. They are not unhappy now.

They are sailing south. In France they stop at L'Orient and Biarritz. In Spain, they visit La Coruna, and in Portugal they stop in Lisbon. The sun gets hotter and they feel good.

Sasha catches a big fish and they eat it for tea.

Soon, they are sailing past Africa. Here, everything is different. They stop in Gambia and people look at them. Small children bring beads and shells and cloth. Tonya buys a green hat. There is a lot of colour and noise and excitement.

They sail for weeks and weeks past Africa. They stop at many small towns and villages by the sea. 'Africa is so interesting, so big,' says Sasha. 'It goes on and on. I look at it on the map, but . . .'

'This is why we are here,' says Jack. 'Talking to different people, seeing different things. The boat, the sea, the wind. Nothing is better than this, is it?'

Some days later they see a big fishing boat. It is moving
very fast.

'Hello!' they shout at the boat. The men on the boat
look at them angrily. Max looks carefully at the boat
through his binoculars.

'There is something wrong with their fishing net,' he
says. Max moves the binoculars and sees something in the
sea. 'I can see some net over there.' He points to their left.
'Why are they leaving it? Let's have a look.'

They get nearer to the net and Tonya takes the binoculars.

'What in the world . . .' says Tonya. 'What's that? There is something in the net. It's alive, but what is it?'

Very slowly they move nearer to the net. The thing in the net is big and it is making a lot of noise.

'I can see it now,' says Tonya. 'It's an orca – a killer whale – and it's hurt. There is blood in the water. What can we do? How can we help it?'

'I can see it too. It is a baby but we must be careful,' says Max.

Jack is in the water. He is carrying a long paddle. 'I am going to help it. I can get the net off its fin,' he says.

'Where's its mother?' asks Sasha. She looks at the sea. 'I can't see any other whales, but they are near here, I think. Be careful, Jack.'

Jack gets the net off the baby killer whale. There is a big cut on its fin, but it swims away. Suddenly there are other killer whales near the boat.

'Jack!' Tonya shouts. 'Get in quickly.' Jack swims to the boat as fast as a fish. 'That baby killer whale . . . I am going to call it Lucky,' he says.

3 The big wave

It begins to rain as they move away from the killer whales. Suddenly it is raining very hard and there is a lot of wind. The sky is black.

Jack says: 'This is bad. We must get away from the wind. I can see a town over there. Let's go.'

'I'm frightened,' says Tonya. It is difficult to hear her because of the wind.

'We're all frightened,' says Jack. 'But everything is OK.'

The town gets nearer but the waves get bigger and bigger. Suddenly a very big wave hits the boat. There is water everywhere.

'Is everyone OK,' shouts Jack. 'Max?'

'Yes,' says Max.

'Sasha?'

'My arm hurts but I'm OK,' says Sasha.

'Tonya? . . . Tonya? . . . Where's Tonya?' shouts Jack.

'She's not in the boat,' says Sasha. 'She's in the water. But where?'

They look in the cold, dark water for hours. 'Tonya! Say
something, Tonya. Where are you?' shouts Max.

The wind gets stronger and the boat is full of water.
Another big wave hits the boat. Sasha's arm hurts a lot
now.

'Jack, we must stop. Do you want us all to die?' says Max. He puts his arm around Jack. 'We can't do any more. Tonya is wearing a lifejacket and she can swim very well. Let's sail to the town.'

Jack puts his head in his hands. 'This can't happen. It can't!' he says.

Max begins to steer the boat. But the wind is too strong. Some time later the boat hits a beach. The three friends get out. They are very tired.

They stop there. Max and Sasha sleep on the beach, but Jack sits near the water. He looks at the sea, thinking about Tonya.

4 Tonya

Tonya is five hundred metres away out in the sea. She begins to swim, but the waves are too big and the water is too cold. She finds some wood and puts her arms around it.

Tonya is thinking: 'I must be strong. I am not going to die. I want to see the sun again. Jack is going to find me.'

Tonya sees a boat far away. She calls to it. 'Help! Help me! I'm over here!' She moves her arms and shouts, but nobody hears her. The wind moves her away from the boat.

'Oh, Jack. I'm sorry,' she says. Her head goes down on to the wood. In the arms of the sea, she sleeps.

Suddenly Tonya is not sleeping. There is no wind and she can see the sun. She looks everywhere. There is a beach in front of her – but she cannot swim to it.

'I am too cold and too tired,' she thinks. 'I must see a boat soon.'

She looks at the sea. There are no boats, no people, but some birds.

'Can the birds help me?' she thinks sleepily.

Tonya listens to the sea. She likes the noise. Then she hears something different.

'Is it a baby crying?' she thinks and looks up.

Ten metres in front of her is a big fin . . . a very big fin. Under the fin is a killer whale. The whale is making the noise. But it is not a baby – it is five metres long. Behind it is another whale. And another. And another.

'Killer whales eat people. I am going to die,' thinks Tonya.

The killer whales come nearer and nearer. Tonya can't feel her legs. 'It's OK, they are cold. That's all,' she thinks. She starts to swim away from the big fins.

'Help me!' she shouts. 'Help, help, help!'

The killer whales are all around her. She closes her eyes and waits.

But she does not die.

The biggest killer whale is under her. Suddenly she is on his back.

'What is happening? Perhaps they are not hungry.' Tonya thinks.

The killer whale moves slowly to the shore. He is taking Tonya to the beach.

Tonya puts her hands on the fin in front of her.

'This is a very big fish – too big for my tea!' she thinks. She smiles and puts her head on his big back. Soon, she is sleeping again.

5 'Tonya? Is that you?'

Jack sits on the beach. The sun is in the sky. Behind him, Max and Sasha sleep.

'I must do something,' he thinks. 'I can't take my boat but I must look for Tonya.'

He begins to walk along the beach. 'There is a town near here. I can get a new boat, then I can look for Tonya.'

Just then Jack sees something on the beach. He walks nearer. It is a woman.

Jack runs to the woman on the beach. 'Tonya?' he shouts. 'Tonya! Is that you?'

Tonya moves her head slowly. 'Jack! Oh, Jack. You're OK!'

Jack puts his arms around Tonya. He kisses her face and cries. He can't speak – he is too happy.

Tonya says: 'What about Max and Sasha? Are they OK, too?'

'Everyone is OK,' answers Jack.

They sit on the beach and look at the sea.

Jack says: 'We are very, very lucky.'

Tonya sits up and sees a small fin in the water. It has a cut on it. The fin waves slowly and moves out to sea. It is waving goodbye, thinks Tonya.

'Lucky. Yes, Lucky,' she says quietly to Jack.

GLOSSARY

around to go round something in a circle

baby a very young animal or person

beach a sandy place at the edge of the sea

business where lots of people work together to make money

catch to take quickly in your hands

cut a knife can cut things

fish an animal that swims in the sea

frighten to make somebody afraid

hurt to be in pain; a broken leg hurts

kiss to touch with your mouth

letter when you write to someone you send them a letter

lifejacket this helps you float on water

lucky when good things happen to you

net people use this to catch fish

sail to travel in a boat

shout to talk loudly

steer to make something go to the left or to the right

strong able to move heavy things; does not break easily

swim to move through water

wave to move your hand in the air; where the sea goes up and down

wind air that moves

world the planet Earth that we live on

Orca

ACTIVITIES

Before Reading

1 Look at the front and back covers. Now answer these questions.

1 How do you think the story ends?   *Yes*   *No*

   a The people on the boat kill the killer whale. ☐ ☐

   b The boat hits ice. ☐ ☐

   c A man shoots a bird. ☐ ☐

   d The killer whale helps a woman. ☐ ☐

2 Where does the story happen?

   a In a small town. ☐ ☐

   b In the mountains. ☐ ☐

   c On an African safari. ☐ ☐

   d At sea. ☐ ☐

3 The boat sails south from England. Which of these does it sail past?

   a Switzerland. ☐ ☐

   b France. ☐ ☐

   c Africa. ☐ ☐

   d Norway. ☐ ☐

4 You are on a boat and you see a killer whale. Do you . . .

   a Move nearer for a better look? ☐ ☐

   b Move away because you are afraid? ☐ ☐

   c Try to catch it in a net? ☐ ☐

While Reading

1 Read pages 1–6 and then answer these questions.

1 Who is Jack's wife?

2 What does Sasha want to see?

3 Where do they want to sail to?

4 Where do they stop in Spain?

5 What do they eat for tea?

2 Read pages 7–12 and then answer these questions.

Who …

1 looks at a boat through binoculars?

2 dives in the water?

3 shouts at Jack?

4 is bleeding?

Where …

5 is the baby killer whale hurt?

6 does Tonya buy a green hat?

7 do they try to sail to in the storm?

8 is the blood?

Why …

9 does the baby killer whale make a noise?

10 does Jack jump in the water?

11 does Tonya shout at Jack?

12 is the sky black?

3 Read pages 13–18. Who says these words?

  1 'My arm hurts.'

  2 'Do you want us all to die?'

  3 'Help me! I'm over here!'

  4 'This can't happen. It can't!'

4 Look at pages 19–24 and then answer these questions.

1 How many birds are there in the picture on page 19?

2 Does Tonya hear a baby crying?

3 What does Jack see on the beach?

4 Why does Jack say, 'We are very, very lucky.'?

5 Look at the picture on page 23 and answer these questions.

1 Where is the boat?

2 Why is Jack running?

3 Find two things in the picture that begin with the letter 'B'.

After Reading

1 Describe what is happening in these pictures.

1

2

3

4

2 Put these sentences in the correct order. Number them 1–6.

a ☐ Jack helps the baby killer whale.

b ☐ The four friends decide to sail around the world.

c ☐ Tonya falls into the water.

d ☐ Jack gives the bird a fish.

e ☐ It begins to rain and there is a lot of wind.

f ☐ Jack sees Tonya on the beach.

3 Are these sentences true or false?

	True	False
1 Jack is married to Sasha.	☐	☐
2 A whale pushes Tonya into the water.	☐	☐
3 The baby killer whale dies in the net.	☐	☐
4 Their boat has a yellow sail.	☐	☐
5 Max is hurt in the storm.	☐	☐

ABOUT THE AUTHORS

Mark Foster and Phillip Burrows have worked as a writer/illustrator team since 1991. They were born three years and many miles apart, but they are very nearly twins. They drive the same car, work on the same computers, and wear the same wellington boots – but not at the same time! They spend all the money they get from writing on gadgets, but please don't tell their wives. Mark and Phill have worked together on several Bookworms titles, including the two thriller and adventure stories *Taxi of Terror* (Starter) and *Escape* (Starter). When they meet to write, they like to go to expensive hotels, eat chips dipped in coffee, and laugh at their own jokes.

OXFORD BOOKWORMS LIBRARY

Classics • Crime & Mystery • Factfiles • Fantasy & Horror
Human Interest • Playscripts • Thriller & Adventure
True Stories • World Stories

The OXFORD BOOKWORMS LIBRARY provides enjoyable reading in English, with a wide range of classic and modern fiction, non-fiction, and plays. It includes original and adapted texts in seven carefully graded language stages, which take learners from beginner to advanced level. An overview is given on the next pages.

All Stage 1 titles are available as audio recordings, as well as over eighty other titles from Starter to Stage 6. All Starters and many titles at Stages 1 to 4 are specially recommended for younger learners. Every Bookworm is illustrated, and Starters and Factfiles have full-colour illustrations.

The OXFORD BOOKWORMS LIBRARY also offers extensive support. Each book contains an introduction to the story, notes about the author, a glossary, and activities. Additional resources include tests and worksheets, and answers for these and for the activities in the books. There is advice on running a class library, using audio recordings, and the many ways of using Oxford Bookworms in reading programmes. Resource materials are available on the website <www.oup.com/elt/gradedreaders>.

The *Oxford Bookworms Collection* is a series for advanced learners. It consists of volumes of short stories by well-known authors, both classic and modern. Texts are not abridged or adapted in any way, but carefully selected to be accessible to the advanced student.

You can find details and a full list of titles in the *Oxford Bookworms Library Catalogue* and *Oxford English Language Teaching Catalogues*, and on the website <www.oup.com/elt/gradedreaders>.

THE OXFORD BOOKWORMS LIBRARY
GRADING AND SAMPLE EXTRACTS

STARTER • 250 HEADWORDS

present simple – present continuous – imperative –
can/cannot, must – *going to* (future) – simple gerunds …

Her phone is ringing – but where is it?

Sally gets out of bed and looks in her bag. No phone. She looks under the bed. No phone. Then she looks behind the door. There is her phone. Sally picks up her phone and answers it. *Sally's Phone*

STAGE 1 • 400 HEADWORDS

… past simple – coordination with *and*, *but*, *or* –
subordination with *before, after, when, because, so* …

I knew him in Persia. He was a famous builder and I worked with him there. For a time I was his friend, but not for long. When he came to Paris, I came after him – I wanted to watch him. He was a very clever, very dangerous man. *The Phantom of the Opera*

STAGE 2 • 700 HEADWORDS

… present perfect – *will* (future) – *(don't) have to, must not, could* –
comparison of adjectives – simple *if* clauses – past continuous –
tag questions – *ask/tell* + infinitive …

While I was writing these words in my diary, I decided what to do. I must try to escape. I shall try to get down the wall outside. The window is high above the ground, but I have to try. I shall take some of the gold with me – if I escape, perhaps it will be helpful later. *Dracula*

STAGE 3 • 1000 HEADWORDS

... should, may – present perfect continuous – *used to* – past perfect –
causative – relative clauses – indirect statements ...

Of course, it was most important that no one should see
Colin, Mary, or Dickon entering the secret garden. So Colin
gave orders to the gardeners that they must all keep away
from that part of the garden in future. *The Secret Garden*

STAGE 4 • 1400 HEADWORDS

... past perfect continuous – passive (simple forms) –
would conditional clauses – indirect questions –
relatives with *where/when* – gerunds after prepositions/phrases ...

I was glad. Now Hyde could not show his face to the world
again. If he did, every honest man in London would be
proud to report him to the police. *Dr Jekyll and Mr Hyde*

STAGE 5 • 1800 HEADWORDS

... future continuous – future perfect –
passive (modals, continuous forms) –
would have conditional clauses – modals + perfect infinitive ...

If he had spoken Estella's name, I would have hit him. I was so
angry with him, and so depressed about my future, that I could
not eat the breakfast. Instead I went straight to the old house.
Great Expectations

STAGE 6 • 2500 HEADWORDS

... passive (infinitives, gerunds) – advanced modal meanings –
clauses of concession, condition

When I stepped up to the piano, I was confident. It was as if I
knew that the prodigy side of me really did exist. And when I
started to play, I was so caught up in how lovely I looked that
I didn't worry how I would sound. *The Joy Luck Club*

Escape

PHILLIP BURROWS AND MARK FOSTER

'I'm not a thief. I'm an innocent man,' shouts Brown. He is angry because he is in prison and the prison guards hate him. Then one day Brown has an idea. It is dangerous – very dangerous.

Taxi of Terror

PHILLIP BURROWS AND MARK FOSTER

'How does it work?' Jack asks when he opens his present – a mobile phone. Later that night, Jack is a prisoner in a taxi in the empty streets of the dark city. He now tries his mobile phone for the first time. Can it save his life?

BOOKWORMS · CRIME & MYSTERY · STARTER

Oranges in the Snow

PHILLIP BURROWS AND MARK FOSTER

'Everything's ready now. We can do the experiment,' says your assistant Joe.

You are the famous scientist Mary Durie working in a laboratory in Alaska. When you discover something very new and valuable, other people want to try to steal your idea – can you stop them before they escape?

BOOKWORMS · FANTASY & HORROR · STARTER

Starman

PHILLIP BURROWS AND MARK FOSTER

The empty centre of Australia. The sun is hot and there are not many people. And when Bill meets a man, alone, standing on an empty road a long way from anywhere, he is surprised and worried.

And Bill is right to be worried. Because there is something strange about the man he meets. Very strange . . .

BOOKWORMS · THRILLER & ADVENTURE · STAGE 1

Goodbye, Mr Hollywood

JOHN ESCOTT

Nick Lortz is sitting outside a café in Whistler, a village in the Canadian mountains, when a stranger comes and sits next to him. She's young, pretty, and has a beautiful smile. Nick is happy to sit and talk with her.

But why does she call Nick 'Mr Hollywood'? Why does she give him a big kiss when she leaves? And who is the man at the next table – the man with short white hair?

Nick learns the answers to these questions three long days later – in a police station on Vancouver Island.

BOOKWORMS · HUMAN INTEREST · STAGE 1

One-Way Ticket – Short Stories

JENNIFER BASSETT

Tom Walsh had a lot to learn about life. He liked travelling, and he was in no hurry. He liked meeting people, anyone and everyone. He liked the two American girls on the train. They were nice and very friendly. They knew a lot of places. Tom thought they were fun. Tom certainly had a lot to learn about life.

This is a collection of short stories about adventures on trains. Strange, wonderful, and frightening things can happen on trains – and all of them happen here.